Balloon on Fire
燃える風船

Haiku and Photos
Edward Levinson

俳句及び写真
エドワード・レビンソン
恵道　Edo

EDWARD LEVINSON
Balloon on Fire

燃える風船

Text and Photos © Edward Levinson, 2019

Cover Photo: Edward Levinson

Published by: Cyberwit.net

ISBN: 978-93-89074-76-5

Touch of Light

Singing a silent song, in a pantomime like dance, light moves freely touching me all over. Tickling the surface of the leaves, penetrating, warming the depths of the earth and my being, light paints its way through nature.

Sitting in the light, its quiet power excites me. It offers me an intoxicating drink, but no glass. I drink with my eyes and fill my inner cup. I look at my life and problems and try to see more clearly the path to take.

Dressing up in the robes of nature, light flirts with me. "Why not drink another cup?" it asks. My eyes smile, the heart laughs, amazed by light's subtle way of courtship.

光と触れあう

光は無音の詩を歌い、パントマイム風ダンスをし、自由に動いて私全体に触れる。光は葉の表面をくすぐり、浸透していき、大地の奥と私の存在を温め、自然に沿って塗り通す。

光の中に座っていると、そのおだやかな力が私を興奮させる。光は酔わせる飲物を私に与えるが、グラスはない。私は眼から飲んで内面のカップを満たす。そして自分の人生と課題を見、どの道を選ぶかをより明確に見ようと試みる。

自然の礼服で正装して、光は私をもてあそぶ。そして言う。「もう一杯飲みませんか?」
光の巧みな求愛の仕方に驚かされて、私は眼にほほえみを浮かべ、こころで笑う。

a hole in the sky
the eye of God opens
I am seen

空に穴神の目が開くぼくを見る
sora ni ana, kami no me ga aku, boku o miru

spring rain
washing heart
spirit's kiss

春雨や心を洗う霊のキス
harusameya, kokoro o arau, rei no kisu

on bare branches
birds constantly chirping
awaiting cherry blossoms

枯枝に鳥鳴き続く桜待ち
kareeda ni, tori naki tsuzuku, sakura machi

spring morning
small bird dances at window
calling me to play

春の朝 窓辺で踊る小鳥「きみ遊ぼう」
haru no asa, madobe de odoru kotori, "kimi asobō"

feeling fine
running with my camera
mountain laughing

元気なぼくカメラと走る山笑う
genki na boku, kamera to hashiru, yama warau

confused on the path
bamboo shoots
show the way

たけのこや行く道悩む知らしめよ
takenoko ya, yukumichi nayamu, shirashimeyo

short nights
dreams birthing poems…
cannot sleep

短夜や夢歌を生む眠れずに
mijikayo ya, yume uta o umu, nemurezu ni

light flickers
rain clouds open
water jewels

雨雲や割れて煌めく水の珠
amagumo ya, warete kirameku, mizu no tama

rainy night
waiting for you
tears of light

雨の夜君を待つ間の光の涙
ame no yoru, kimi o matsumano, hikari no namida

climbing a tree
fine day feeling fine courageous
lopping limbs

木登りや天気元気勇気の枝おろし
ki nobori ya, tenki genki yūki no, eda oroshi

pulling weeds
mosquitoes on my back
have a picnic

草取りや僕の背で蚊のピクニック
kusa tori ya, boku no se de ka no, pikuniku

tilling paddy
old woman totters
pampas grass sways

田を 起こす老婆ふらふらすすき揺れ
ta o okosu, rōba furafura, susuki yure

play in dirt, boy
work with dirt, man
sleep on dirt, dog

土と遊ぶ、坊や
土で働く、男
土に寝る、犬

tsuchi to asobu, bōya
tsuchi de hataraku, otoko
tsuchi ni neru, inu

warm sun after rain
frogs awaken
winter withers

雨後日差す蛙目覚める冬なごむ
ugo hizasu, kawazu mezameru, fuyu nagomu

spring buds…
clenched fists waiting
to break open

閉じて 待つ春の芽 拳こじ開けよ
tojite matsu, haru no me, kobushi kojiakeyo

spring sunset
floats freely
balloon on fire

春夕日燃える風船ゆるり浮かぶ
haru yūhi, moeru fūsen, yururi ukabu

cloudy day...
shining persimmon
lives in heart

曇り日や 柿輝いて胸にあり
kumoribi ya, kaki kagayaite, mune ni ari

lonely branch
dove touches down for a moment
in early morning mist

枝 寂し鳩ひと休み朝の靄
eda sabishi, hato hitoyasumi, asa no moya

two dragonflies
linked in flight
united in love

トンボ二匹 連なって飛ぶ愛結び
tonbo ni-hiki, tsuranatte tobu, ai musubi

after the rain
sun dances
across blue sky
spinning me
its partner

雨上がり
太陽踊る
青空渡る
僕パートナー
スピニング

ame agari, taiyo odoru, aozora wataru,
boku pātonā, supiningu

sunset ball
drops into paddy water
striking heart

夕日の球水田に落つ胸叩く
yūhi no tama, suiden ni otsu, mune tataku

fall clouds
sage's beard grows
time flows

秋の雲賢者の髭伸び時流る
aki no kumo, kenja no hige nobi, toki nagaru

star shaped
pumpkin flowers
radiant humans

花カボチャ星に輝く人のごと
hana kabocha, hoshi ni kagayaku, hito no goto

full of heaven's rain
heads bow to the earth…
hydrangea flowers

天水に頭地に垂るあじさいの花
tensui ni, kōbe chi ni taru, ajisai no hana

at the road's edge
five snake gourds
protecting mountains

道の端からすうり五個 山護る
michi no hashi, karasu uri go-ko, yama mamoru

morning dew
voices of the frogs
toning down

朝露や蛙の声の低くなり
asa tsuyu ya, kaeru no koe no, hikuku nari

Clouds dance
Frogs sing
Moon warns
Earth quakes
Stillness comes
Special moment

雲踊る
蛙歌う
月告げる
地が揺れる
静止する
神秘のとき

kumo odoru, kaeru utau, tsuki tsugeru,
chi ga yureru, seishi suru, shinpi no toki

window of light
on stone floor
Buddha appears

光の窓石床に映え仏現る
hikari no mado, ishiyuka ni hae, hotoke arawaru

sitting in lotus position
Zen carpenter
hammers nails
along long hall of his life

蓮華座組む
禅の大工
釘を打つ
長い人生の廊下に沿って

renge-za kumi, Zen no daiku, kugi o utsu,
nagai jinsei no rōka ni sotte

bird's song
worries gone
fly away

鳥の歌案ずること無し飛んで行く
tori no uta, anzuru koto nashi, tonde iku

spider dances for breakfast
insects call to prayer
cicadas vibrate mind

朝食を求めて躍る蜘蛛
祈りに招く虫
こころ震わす蝉

chōshoku o motomete odoru kumo
inori ni maneku mushi
kokoro furuwasu semi

waves of Light
wrapping Body
soothing Soul

光の波 体覆って魂癒す
hikari no nami, karada ōtte, tamashii iyasu

gingko leaf
floats to the ground
homecoming

銀杏の葉地上に散りて里帰り
ichō no ha, chijō ni chirite, satogaeri

evening sunlight
glimmers on tree leaves
becoming stars

夕べの陽 木の葉にきらり星となる
yūbe no hi, konoha ni kirari, hoshi to naru

crying insects
distant dog howls
equinox cometh

鳴く虫や犬の遠吠え彼岸来る
naku mushi ya, inu no tōboe, higan kuru

crisp night
sharp crescent moon
cuts heart

夜気きりり鋭い三日月心切る
yaki kiriri, surudoi mikazuki, kokoro kiru

fall wind
takes the unknown road
spreading wings

秋の風 未知の道行く翼伸ばす
aki no kaze, michi no michiyuku, tsubasa nobasu

north wind
touches my shoulder
awakening dreams

北の風 ぼくの肩触れ夢起こす
kita no kaze, boku no kata fure, yume okosu

new year
flows into Ginza
with money

元旦の銀座に流れる金もまた
gantan no, Ginza ni nagareru, kane mo mata

standing straight
amidst city confusion
slender leek flower

直立す 混乱の町に韮の花
chokuritsu su, konran no machi ni, nira no hana

maple trees
in building's lobby
imitating nature

カエデの木ビルのロビーに自然模す
kaede no ki, biru no robī ni, shizen mosu

big soba bowl
chipped on rim
chopsticks resting

蕎麦丼縁に欠け有り箸を掛け
soba donburi, fuchi ni kake ari, hashi o kake

from leftovers
wife's rice porridge
no complaints

残り物妻の雑炊文句なし
nokori mono, tsuma no zōsui, monku nashi

inn's waterfall…
in sake flask
drops remaining

宿の滝徳利数滴残り酒
yado no taki, tokuri suuteki, nokori sake

pink ladies
smile in hot sun
cotton roses

ピンクレディース猛暑に笑顔花芙蓉
pinku redīzu, moshō ni egao, hana fuyō

peony garden
world of color
Harmonic Peace

牡丹苑世界の色や令和なり
*botan en, sekai no iro ya, **Reiwa nari***

cold day blossoms
cafe sunset
tastes sweet

花冷えや日没のカフェ甘味あり
hanabie ya, nichibotsu no cafe, kanmi ari

Angry clouds
Surround destroyed school and village
Sun's face pops out
To say hello... goodbye

怒る雲
囲む破壊の学校と村
太陽ちらりと顔を出し
告げるこんにちは　さようなら

ikari no kumo,
kakomu kaimetsu no gakkō to mura
taiyō chirarito kao o dashi
tsugeru kon'nichiwa… sayōnara

In memory of the Ōkawa Elementary School tragedy during the Tohoku Earthquake Tsunami Disaster 2011, written when I visited the site.

「怒る雲」の句は、2011年3月、東日本大震災の被災地、石巻市大川小学校へ弔問に訪れた時の句。

on Buddha's birthday
a trip to disaster zone
souls in the wind

仏生会被災地の旅風に霊
butsushōe, hisaichi no tabi, kaze ni rei

winter storm
retreat to darkroom
beauty surfaces

冬嵐籠もる暗室美女浮かぶ
fuyu arashi, komoru anshitsu, bijo ukabu

first days of spring
sun and clouds
battle on

立春や太陽と雲闘えり
risshun ya, taiyō to kumo, tatakaeri

cicadas crying
heart worrying…
can I succeed?

蝉叫ぶ悩むこころや勝てるかな？
semi sakebu, kokoro nayamu ya, kateru kana?

piercing garden
deep in me too
fall morning sun

庭に射す我にも深く秋朝日
niwa ni sasu, ware ni mo fukaku, aki asahi

silver crescent moon
walk on the edge
curve of life

銀三日月人生のカーブ端歩く
gin mikadzuki, jinsei no kābu, hashi aruku,

Thoughts on Haiku

Having lived in Japan for 40 years I feel I know it well. I often wonder if certain of my haiku will only have meaning for Japanese readers and people familiar with Japanese culture? Does it have international appeal to bridge cultures? More importantly, can a traditional short three line haiku (with or without a *kigo* seasonal word) have universal meaning and share something special with the world?

Most of my haiku come to me in inspirational moments felt through the senses: sitting or walking in nature, on trains, even while driving. I quickly scribble them down in elementary Japanese using the Roman alphabet, and then render them into English while working on the Japanese *kanji* to make it more poetic. My original inspirations usually include *kigo*, but I try not to intellectually force them into the poem. Some of the haiku are written in the free-style with extra syllables and extra lines in Japanese while still honoring the brevity of the traditional form.

Through these haiku and photos, I hope we can cross bridges together.

私の作句法

日本在住40年の私は、日本を良く分かっていると思っている。だが、時として、私の作る俳句というものが、日本人の読者にだけ、または日本文化と親しんでいる人々だけに意議のあることか？　と疑問に思うことがある。さまざまな文化に橋をかける、国際的なアッピールになっているだろうか？　と。

より重要なことは、伝統的な5-7-5の俳句（季語の有無を問わず）は、何か特別なものを世界中で分かち合う、普遍的な意味をもっているか、ということである。

私の俳句のほとんど全ては、感覚が感じ取った瞬間のインスピレーションから生まれる、歩いたり坐ったりする自然の中、電車の中、ドライブ中に。私は急いでまず、日本語の言葉をローマ字で書く。それからその句を英語に変えながら、より詩的に直して日本語の漢字で書く。私の発想の源は常に季語を含んでいる。だが私は季語を詩句の中に、知識でもって無理矢理押し込むことは避けている。私の日本語の俳句は、字余りや字足らず、句またがりなどのフリースタイルで書かれている。だが、なお私は、日本の伝統的形式の簡潔さを尊重しているのである。

本書の俳句や写真を通して、皆共に、橋を渡ることが出来ることを私は願っている。

Acknowledgments

I started writing haiku in the late 1980's. In 1990, with beginner skills, I entered a few haiku in the famous "Itoen O–i Ocha New Haiku Award" competition, which received 40,000 entries. To my surprise, my haiku "north wind" (p.40) received a Special Award for Haiku in English. This gave me confidence to keep writing. Many thanks to all those who have listened to my live readings, read or published my haiku in books and journals. I am truly grateful for all the support and encouraging feedback I receive.

I would like to thank the following individuals:

Ban'ya Natsuishi (Masayuki Inui) – Haiku Poet, Chair of the World Haiku Association and Conference, Professor at Meiji University
Noriko Mizusaki – Poet, Chair of Pandora Poetry Group and Pandora Journal – Professor at Komazawa University
Scott Watson – Poet, Poetry Publisher, Professor at Tohoku Gakuin University

Shizuka Tsuruta – author, my partner and collaborator for many years - for her continuous help in life, for making thoughtful suggestions and checking the final Japanese.

Special thanks to:
Dr. Karunesh Kumar Agrawal, Managing Editor at Cyberwit

Edward Levinson, September 2019
Haiku Pen Name: Edo (恵道): *megumi no michi*, from kanji characters meaning Road of Blessings

謝辞

私が初めて俳句を作ったのは1980年代末の東京でした。それ以来今日まで、拙句を著書や雑誌でお読み下さり、朗読会でお聴き下さった皆様にお礼を申し上げます。実は、作句初期の1990年「伊藤園　おーいお茶新俳句大賞」(全4万句の応募・審査員金子兜太氏他)に数句を応募したら、「北の風」(p40)の句が「伊藤園特別賞-英作賞)」を受賞しました。このことは、素人の私に、作句の勇気を与えてくれました。皆様のサポートと激励に心から感謝申し上げます。

多大なお力添えを頂いた次の方々に心より深謝致します。

夏石番矢(乾昌幸)氏　俳人　NPO 世界俳句協会理事長
　　　　　　　　　明治大学教授

水崎野里子氏　詩人・歌人「パンドラ・PANDORA」主宰
　　　　　　　　駒澤大学講師

スコット・ワトソン氏　詩人　詩集編集出版人
　　　　　　　　　東北学院大学教授

鶴田 静　文筆家　私の仕事と生活を支えている私の伴侶。句作歴10年。本書の最終添削助言者。日本文藝家協会・日本ペンクラブ会員

スペシャル・サンクス
Dr. Karunesh Kumar Agrawal氏　Cyberwit出版 編集長
本書の出版に厚くお礼申し上げます。

エドワード・レビンソン　俳号：恵道（えど、恵みの道）
2019年9月

Edward Levinson is an American photographer, essayist, and poet living in Japan since 1979.

His photo book *Timescapes Japan* received a First Prize Award in one of the categories of the Prix de la Photographie Paris 2007. His short pinhole movie *Tokyo Story* was an Official Selection at six film competitions, winning several awards.

Writing publications include: *Whisper of the Land* (Fine Line Press 2014), a collection of essays based on his life in Japan; and two essay books in Japanese (Iwanami Shoten 2011, 2007). His haiku and poetry appear in a variety of books, magazines, and journals.

Edward's photographs have been regularly exhibited in Japan, the U.S.A., and Europe and are in various museum and private collections. He is a member of The Photographic Society of Japan and The Japan P.E.N. Club.

He lives in the countryside in Kamogawa, Chiba Prefecture where has a studio gallery and keeps a natural garden, a source of much inspiration.

Please visit:
http://www.edophoto.com
http://www.whisperoftheland.com

エドワード・レビンソン
Edward Levinson

1953年米国生まれ。バージニア州立コモンウェルス大学
で写真を学ぶ。1979年来日。写真家として写真展国内外
開催多数。

ピンホール・カメラによる短編映画「東京ストーリー
(2014年)」が6件の映画コンペに入選。現在続編を制作
中。写真集『タイムスケープス・ジャパン』（日本カメ
ラ社。07年度パリ写真賞部門別1位）、他。

エッセイ『エドさんのピンホール写真教室』
『ぼくの植え方』（ともに岩波書店刊）。
『Whisper of the Land』（Fine Line Press）。その他多
数の書籍と新聞・雑誌に写真と記事を寄稿。詩作と作句
に励み、作品が種々の雑誌や自著に掲載。

千葉県鴨川市の自宅に自らナチュラル・ガーデンを築き
創造の源泉の一部としている。
日本ペンクラブ会員　日本写真協会会員

http://www.edophoto.com/jp